The Pink Unicorns

of

Male Breast Cancer

ISBN: 978-0-9956006-0-7

First Published in 2016 by Blossom Spring Publishing.

www.blossomspringpublishing.com

The Pink Unicorns of Male Breast Cancer © 2016

Alan F. Herbert.

Alan F. Herbert has asserted his right under the Copyright,
Designs and Patents

Act, 1988, to be identified as Author of this Work.

British Library Cataloguing in Publication Data.

A catalogue record for this book is available from the
British Library.

Acknowledgement

Many thanks for the assistance of
Stichting Jij Speelt De Hoofdrol and het
Borstkankersymposium, www.borstkankersymposium.nl,
The Netherlands.

INDEX

THE PINK UNICORNS OF MALE BREAST CANCER

The Pink Unicorns

of

Male Breast Cancer

Written by

Alan F. Herbert

Forward

The Pink Unicorns of Male Breast Cancer is the story of my journey through breast cancer. Yes, with breast cancer. No, not bone cancer or prostate cancer. Breast cancer, you know, all that pink ribbon stuff.

This little preamble is to underline the normal reaction I get when I tell someone I had breast cancer. First, they think they misheard me. Add to that, the looks of suspicion, suspicion of a very bad joke, pure disbelief, and finally complete mental confusion. This is the reaction of many when taking in the mortality rate for men from the disease. With the acute lack of interest in the general media, one British cancer organisation stated: "There were too few men, therefore, women have priority." In simple terms, men are less important. When all is added together, you will begin to understand why this story needs to be told.

The treatment of cancer is truly holistic. It is very individual in how it affects each person and their world. I don't intend this story to be about the various cancer treatments; just my story and how I experienced it.

My wide-ranging life experience and medical knowledge did not prepare me for the shock of late February 2012, although I was prepared in that I was reasonably fit at the time of my diagnosis. I was losing some excess weight and getting back into training for a marathon.

I had a knowledge of cancer treatments and the associated surgery. This was backed up with the black humour of nursing combined with that of the Royal Navy Submarine Service.

All of this came together and was much needed to get me through male breast cancer.

There is little information to look up about male breast cancer. It is easier to join Monty Python in looking for the Holy Grail. My medical encyclopedia doesn't even use the word "male" anywhere in its information on the diagnosis, treatment, and statistics about breast cancer. It only has information about women with the disease. Another cancer organisation's total input is "men can also get breast cancer." Just six words to cover the shock of becoming a Pink Unicorn.

Why a unicorn? The unicorn is a mythical beast. We male breast cancer survivors are truly mythical; the majority of people don't know or believe we exist. We are so rare that some doctors don't even consider breast cancer as a male diagnosis. Misdiagnosis may be as high as 40%. This sad fact often has fatal consequences when it combines with ignorance of the general public.

Everything to do with breast cancer is covered in a pretty pink fog, although truly there is nothing pink or pretty about breast cancer. We unicorns just had to be pink as that is the media colour of breast cancer.

If you want some figures, I am one of one in 100,000 men and form just 0.02% of all male cancers, and 0.9% of breast cancer cases are diagnosed in males. This all means about 2,000 Americans, 400 British, 100 Dutch, and 40 Swedish men per year will be told "you have breast cancer." The majority will be in the late stage 3 or too late stage 4 of the disease having already spread into the body when diagnosed. A quarter of those diagnosed will die from the disease. I don't know if I should belong to the 400 British or the 100 Dutch; it doesn't really matter.

Relatively speaking, more men die from breast cancer than women--25% as opposed to 19%. While the disease is easier to detect by men and easier to treat, cancer travels through the body much quicker in men. Therefore, early detection is vital, but how can there be early detection if men don't even know they can get the disease?

After nearly forty years in nursing, I only vaguely knew that men could get it. I had no details, simply that men could get it, but it was very rare. So come, travel my road, it might save someone's grandad.

What's This Lump?

Somewhere around February 24th, 2012, I was laying half awake in my bed. My left nipple was itching. Sleepily, I gently scratched it and felt a small hard lump just above the nipple. The lump was quite firm but painless. Although very curious, I went back to sleep. I didn't know then that itching and dry flaky skin around the areola are some of the early signs of breast cancer in men.

In the morning, I checked again. I found a smooth rubbery lump about the same texture as a pencil rubber. It only affected one small area (not the whole nipple), and it wasn't tender so I knew it wasn't mastitis. As a long-distance runner and former Judoka, nipple rub and mastitis are things I knew. This wasn't either although I had recently stepped up my running training for the Berenloop Marathon on Terschelling in the coming November.

I waited for a couple of days to see what it did--it didn't do anything. It wasn't hot, it wasn't sore, it didn't get worse, but it didn't get better. My medical knowledge exhausted, I went to see the doctor. I was thinking it was possibly a cyst caused by chronic nipple rub from my running.

My doctor examined me, washed her hands, and turned to me.

"I don't think it is cancer, but I'm sending you for a mammogram just to be sure."

Cancer? That thought hadn't even crossed my mind. She added that if she thought it was cancer, she would have sent me directly to the surgeon but that the lump was smooth.

So a couple of days later, I am sat outside the mammogram unit at the Antonius Hospital in Sneek along with several anxious-faced women and their husbands with equally drawn faces. I was getting a few sideways curious glances as I was a man, and I was there alone.

I was called in by a slightly bemused radiographer and watched by even more bemused patients.

Well, we had fun. The poor radiographers were trying so hard to be professional. That doesn't work with me. A male mammogram is a cross between twister and catch the wet soap, but eventually, they were successful. I was asked to wait in the changing cubicle as they wanted to do an echo as well.

Gentlemen, I will assure you my heart goes out to all the ladies. A mammogram is decidedly not pleasant.

I was called back in and noted an immediate change in the atmosphere. It had gone back to the strict professionals. The fun was over. Another technician came in to do the echo, but first they had to shave the area. I got the impression it was probably another first for them, shaving a breast prior to an echo. This was obvious from their dexterity with a razor. Then it was followed up with a biopsy. No one had said anything about a biopsy!

I have suffered a few "nipple twisters" in my time, but a biopsy is really something else. It's like someone striking a match inside your breast. That was followed by taking some lymphatic fluid which ached like nothing I have ever known before. In short, it hurt. I asked the technician, strictly off the record being an ex-nurse, what the score was. He said 50/50. He lied.

That evening after I got home and showered, I stood in front of the mirror and took a really good look and there were the faint signs of breast cancer I knew. The slight difference was in the nipples. The left areola was a bit sunken and the nipple misshapen, but it was very slight. When I showered, I couldn't feel the lump with the flat hand even though I knew it was there. It had to be a fingertip search.

The immortal phrase of Apollo 13 went through my mind. "Houston, we have a problem"--cool, clear, matter of fact. There was a problem that needed fixing. In Naval terminology, I was in deep.

I had been given an appointment to see the surgeon on March 5th for the results. When I put it all together, the mood changed. The sudden unannounced biopsy, the technician's reply, and my own observations. In my heart, I already knew the results. I had to talk to my kids.

How do you say "Hi kids, it looks like I have cancer," when you have just come back into their lives after being away for ten years in a different country?

I simply told them what had been going on--all about the lump that shouldn't be there, and that I didn't think things were good. I was a medic. I find no point in bull. No rose tints. Just straight facts. It gives people time to get ready in their own minds and also to make any plans they need to. You can only work with the truth.

In the meantime, I started my search for information about male breast cancer beginning with my own medical books. In a word, zilch, the square root of zero. After that, I started searching the internet. You find a snippet here and a snippet there. It seemed to me that cancer organisations have either nothing or some small amount that requires another oncologist to understand it. The internet is worldwide. The most information I have about male breast cancer came from an American site, but that was found after my surgery and during my chemotherapy. From that site, I learnt how to do a fingertip check just like the ladies do. I learnt that the normal age of onset is fifty-five to seventy. Signs include itching and dry flaky skin. I had the dry skin a few weeks previous. Later comes the misshapen, sunken, and discharging nipples which you can read about in the female signs and symptoms which are published on all the other sites concerning breast cancer. Although when you start showing those later signs as a man, let's just say you are in very deep trouble. The lump is usually located below the nipple, mine was above.

You also begin to ask yourself. How? When? What? Where? Why?

I remembered one evening about three years earlier, my fiancée and I were having a rare little intimate moment, and she found a lump in my breast. It was a little sore when pressed. I was also busy with running training at the time. I put it down to irritation from running; it wasn't painful unless pressed and didn't get worse. I thought it was a little mastitis. It was simply forgotten about. My fiancée was terminally ill with a lung disease and disabled with severe rheumatoid arthritis so a little mastitis is really rather insignificant. Was this the same lump as then? I don't know. I will guess it probably was.

The how? Initially, I put it down to constant irritation from running. Although if this was so, breast cancer would be more prevalent with long-distance runners and it isn't. Later, I read that there are three recognised causes: genetics, hormonal, and radiation. Genetically, there is no known history of any form of cancer in either side of the family. I have since had a full study by the University Medical Centre Groningen, and they can find absolutely no genetic cause for breast cancer or, in fact, any cancer in my genes. My hormones are normal. I do not have Klinefelter's syndrome. Radiation? Yes, I had worked with radiation for five years in the Royal Navy. I had never exceeded any dose; in fact, my life dose hadn't reached my annual limit, and I had never been exposed to anything high level. Or had I?

I remembered being ordered to make an emergency reactor compartment entry for exercise purposes aboard HMS/M Renown. I was ordered to make an actual entry and complete a radiation survey down to the lower level. Exposing anyone unnecessarily like this to ionising radiation is, in fact, against international radiation law. You can try telling that to a lieutenant commander who wants to make exercises as realistic as possible.

After I had done the survey, I told the engineers that I hadn't heard the control rods drop. They told me that they hadn't dropped the control rods which absorb the neutrons and stop criticality! They had been ordered to just turn the power right down low so that they could make a fast recovery after the entry was complete. That meant all the time I was in that reactor compartment, the reactor was still critical, and I had certainly too high energy Gamma radiation. Yes, that would cause it... Thank you, lieutenant commander FG. I hope your guitar goes permanently out of tune, all your strings break, and you forget the words of "Greenback Dollar"! He never really understood anything about radiation anyway. All I could do was wait for the results from the mammogram, echo, and biopsy. Until then, life continued as normal. You can't do anything with what if's. All I had was an almost certainty I had a disease that I could find no information on.

The Day My World Changed Forever

March 5th, 2012. D-day. First thing that morning, I had a meeting with the jobcentre. It seemed they may have finally found a job for me as an industrial first-aid instructor. I had to give up my nursing registration when I became fulltime carer for my late fiancée. I hadn't been able to do the required continuation studies to keep up my registration. The job looked promising. I didn't have the required papers but had plenty of experience. I had been trained to a very high level in the Royal Navy. I had given lectures and trained first-aid parties on board ship. I had also been part of the Dutch Red Cross disaster team for North Nederland. Getting my instructor's certificate would be fairly basic.

So there I was sitting in the surgical waiting room with my daughter waiting to see the surgeon. Once again, I was surrounded by ladies, most with their husbands, all with drawn faces. Their minds tying themselves in knots and wondering if.

I was already certain of the results.

We were called in, and the surgeon was wearing a serious face and being very correct. I told her I was quite okay with the situation.

The results. In simple terms, the tumour was malignant and the lymph glands had also tested positive. The former I had expected; the latter, shall I say, was rather disappointing. I was then immediately dispatched for liver, lungs, and a bone scan.

Little did I know how much the simple sentence, "You have cancer, and it's malignant," does to your life.

Everywhere I went, all was explained in very simple terms despite my telling them I was an ex-nurse. Knowledge in this case really is power as only the unknown causes fear. I had worked in the operating theatre, seen the operation worked on a breast surgery ward, and run an oncology clinic.

So the information. I have breast cancer. It is malignant, and it has spread. The question now being how far? I had recently had a liver scan, and that had come back clear so I could assume it was probably still okay. This is the "waiting for results." It is pure torment. You know you have cancer so you want to get going and get it sorted, but you must wait patiently. All the time your mind is doing handsprings, and everyone that cares about you is also in a blue funk.

A week later, once more by the surgeon. Again she wore the serious face. My liver and lung scans had come back clear. That was good. The bone scan showed two hot spots on my ribs.

Now was my time to panic. Bone cancer is scary stuff. It is very difficult to treat. Often there are periods of remission only for it to reappear again. I had lost three friends to that in the past. It is not pleasant.

I was sent off for a detailed x-ray. Again, the wait for results. Until everything was cut and dried, they would not give me any information, not even a pencil line plan, no prognosis. All I had was a diagnosis and a hundred unanswered questions doing gymnastics in my brain.

This is, in fact, the worst time to my mind as there is so much uncertainty. All you do know is you have cancer.

Eventually, the results were all in. The detailed scan was clear. The surgeon had a happy face on and showed me the picture of the scan, and I told her exactly what the cause of the hot spots was. On February 16th, I had crashed on my motorcycle. The hot spots were from the straps on my jacket that pulled tight when I hit the ground at 50 mph. That's why you should always wear the correct protective gear. If I hadn't been, I would have spent weeks in the hospital with several open fractures instead of walking away with some bruises and pulled muscles but still passing the job interview the next morning. A possible job that had just become merely academic under the new circumstances.

My smile was back. Yes, I could smile again. I am still smiling. I am a man plus I was "Jack" and a submariner. Let's be really honest. Breast cancer isn't the same traumatic disaster for a man as it is for a woman.

My breasts haven't been a major factor in my life since I was about nine or ten years old. They mean nothing to my manliness. I haven't been finding the best way to show them off to attract a mate or dominate a rival for most of my adult life. They have absolutely no function for me as a man. They are merely some small masses of redundant tissue. Therefore, those psychological aspects of breast cancer for me are minimal. Yes, I have cancer. It's stage 3 and has spread into the lymph glands. That is scary, but it can be treated. The plan is finally unveiled. Initially, surgery--a mastectomy and lymph node toilet. This will probably be followed up with chemotherapy and/or radiotherapy depending on the laboratory results following the surgery.

The medical staff have an easy time with me as I am not terrified by it all, and I still have a sense of humour. The mammacare nurses think I am great. Well, I suppose they should, after all, I'm the only man they have on their books.

Bye Bye Booby

April 11th, 2012. The first strike. Surgery. Lisa came with me to the Antonius Hospital as I went for my operation. It used to be called a radical mastectomy. I have seen this operation several times in the operating theatre so no real worries. Again, no problems with the staff explaining it all to me.

The boys couldn't be with me. They were on their way to Singapore for five weeks' work. There were only two slight problems. My bed had been marked up for "Mrs. Herbert" and the room--it was the same ward, same room, and same bed my daughter, Lisa, had when a minor operation went very seriously wrong.

The staff understood the reluctance, and I was given a new room directly. Once I settled in, signed all the papers, and was told all over again about the operation, I seemed to have fallen asleep. I barely remember going down to theatre. I found that sad as I normally have a joke or two with the theatre staff before going to sleep. Mind you, they had a laugh anyway. Lisa had got a pair of gloves, filled the fingers with toilet paper and put them on my feet. Surprise when they took my blanket off!

I woke up back in my room. A little while later, Lisa came back. There had been no problems and everything had gone smoothly. She was so very relieved. Her simple op had turned into six weeks in intensive care and three visits to the operating theatre. My going to the Antonius Hospital had been a leap of faith for both of us. She must have been going through hell while I was in the operating theatre. I decided to get my head down again. Well, more likely the pain control decided for me. The next morning everything was in order. There had been no haemorrhaging. The drains had little fluid in them and were removed. With the ladies, the drains tend to remain in for a week or more. The dressings were changed and a pressure bandage applied. I was surprised to find I had been given my own chain mail vest. The surgeon had used clips not sutures. Seems she changed her mind as when we talked about the operation, she had said she would use sutures, but I was happy. I had a huge but neat operation wound. The tumour was gone as was my left nipple along with eighteen lymph glands so I learnt later.

Once again, I had to wait for the results. Ten days later, I went see the surgeon to get the clips removed and the results. The clips came out easily and the wound was well healed. And the results?

Those were not so good. The tumour was a stage three invasive ductal carcinoma. Twelve of the eighteen lymph glands were also affected, including the top or sentinel lymph gland. This is next to the main artery so although neither the tumour nor lymph glands had yet developed their own blood supply, the chance of any stray cancer cells sculling around in my body was considerably increased. It was time to meet the oncologist and learn the next part of the plan.

The Oncologist
OR THE MASTER POISONER

Once again, my daughter, Lisa, went with me. My oncologist is fairly abrupt in his manner, but that's fine with me. I was given a thorough examination including my height and weight but didn't need to go for a pre-chemotherapy E.C.G. as I had one a few months earlier. I had needed cardioversion when I developed atrial fibrillation. The follow-up by the heart specialist had given me a clean bill of health and permission to run another marathon. My heart was that good.

My oncologist went through the laboratory findings with me. Apparently, it was quite an aggressive tumour which was an oestrogen feeder. Yes, I am a normal man, and we men also produce a small amount of oestrogen. Being an aggressive tumour, I was lucky that it had been starved if I had it as long as I suspected.

I am to receive chemotherapy followed by radiotherapy combined with hormone therapy. The chemotherapy would be six doses at three week intervals commencing on May 9th. Three times a triple of five fluorouracil (F), Epirubicin (E), and Cyclofosfamide (C) (F.E.C.), three times with Docotaxel (Taxotere), and a follow up with Tamoxafin, an oestrogen suppressant.

We were seen by the oncology nurse who gave us more information to read up on after telling me not to take any medications other than those I was on and to stop dieting immediately. Pity, it was going great. I had got down to 82 kgs.

F.E.C. has ten common side effects. It attacks the bone marrow hitting the red and white blood cell production resulting in anaemia and a lowered immune system. Also, it can cause diarrhoea, nausea and vomiting, and hair loss. It can damage the heart muscle, cause a painful mouth and lips, tiredness, and coloured urine.

Taxotere has twenty-two side effects. This, too, hits the bone marrow damaging red and white blood cells. It lowers blood pressure and causes both diarrhoea and constipation. Additionally, it can cause flu-like symptoms and muscular pain, hair loss, dry skin, itching, skin rashes, skin colouration, fever on the day of administration, loss of strength, breathlessness, nausea and vomiting, sore mouth and lips, eye irritation, allergy, alteration or loss of taste, fluid retention, tiredness, and loss of peripheral sensation. So select any or all at any severity. What did I know about chemo? It makes you sick and your hair falls out. Now I had a bit more of an idea what chemo really meant. I will admit the idea of being "poorly" for weeks at a time was scary. Could I handle it? I would soon find out.

It looked like the summer would be a bit of compromise...

General Thoughts

While undergoing all this, I had naturally continued my search for information. I found out that the general media have transformed breast cancer almost completely into a woman's disease in the same class as ovarian or cervical cancer.

I'll ask three simple questions:

1. How many women don't know they can get breast cancer?

2. How many men don't know they can get breast cancer?

3. How many women don't know their men can get breast cancer?

Now compare the answers. There's something seriously wrong, isn't there?

The amount of information for men about the disease ranks along with that of hen's teeth or rocking horse pooh to use Naval terminology.

Statistics given by various organisations concerning male breast cancer are also varying and in some cases, non-existent. One cancer organisation combines both male and female breast cancer figures. Here in the Netherlands, the ratio is about 14,000 women to 85 men per year.

In general, the global ratio is somewhere between 0.65 % to 0.9%. My oncologist quoted 1 in 200 or 0.5%, but it's very rare affecting around 1 in 100,000 men and makes up just 0.2% of all male cancers.

The incidence of male breast cancer has been slowly increasing over the past twenty-five years according to several cancer organisations, and the age of onset also appears to be dropping. I recently heard of another Pink Unicorn losing the battle at age forty-two. That's thirteen years before the normal onset of the disease. So no matter what your age, don't be complacent. Check those pects! Men do not get routine mammograms!

This is merely the tip of the iceberg. All the information in the folders handed out to breast cancer patients is aimed at women. In one folder I was given, it had one page about the disease and treatments and five pages about wigs, prosthesis, special bras, reconstruction, and implants. As to the recovery time needed before returning to work, the work envisaged being hoovering, doing the wash and later light gardening. All the line drawings regarding post-operative exercises are of a woman.

Very little of the information is of any use to an active man. A question like how will this affect me trekking through mountains with a heavy rucksack got me a blank stare as an answer.

I read an online article from British cancer research about having a nipple tattoo. I have since seen some, and they are good, but my mammacare nurses found that this is contra indicated due to the damage to my lymphatics. This information was on a cancer research site. So you also get conflicting information--one group of experts saying you can have a tattoo, the other group of experts saying no way, no tattoos, far too dangerous!

I suppose one of the plus points about it all is that you get treated a bit special, but the step into the breast cancer man's world is very difficult for many medical staff; that is, if they even get over the initial shock of meeting a real live Pink Unicorn.

What's Your Poison?

May 9th, 2012. The first dose of chemo and a cocktail of F.E.C. I took the pre-med, anti-emetic, and went to the hospital. Lisa, Collin, and I checked into the ward. I had my bloods checked a few days before. The receptionist double-checked everything thinking there was some computer error as there was supposed to be a breast cancer patient there for treatment, but it was a man standing in front of her. Once she was convinced it was all correct quietly blushing and apologetic, she assigned me to a room.

Along came a nurse and explained to me once again all that would be happening. She asked if I had any problems about it all. I told her the truth--I was a bit apprehensive as I am an active person. I don't do sick and normally function at 110% of normal people. I rarely, sorry, very rarely, took painkillers or anything else, occasionally some eye drops and a nasal decongestant or drops for sinusitis to which I am prone. I eat a good varied diet cooked from scratch so I have no vitamin or mineral supplement requirements.

This was all about to go out of the window. To what level I had no idea.

The nurse wanted to know how I felt about losing my hair? *I am a man! I am already going bald and have been for years. What's the big deal?*

Once again, we had stepped back into the woman's world. The hair, is a woman's crowning glory ever since her mummy first put a ribbon in it. For a woman, losing her hair is an absolute disaster; for us men it is well, normal.

A barber once told me men either go grey or bald. If you go grey first, you keep your hair; if you start losing your hair and then go grey, say bye bye to it. Whichever starts first, wins.

If that side effect really kicks in, I will probably have less hair on my body than I did as a new born baby so still an element of fun.

I was given an anti-emetic by I/V infusion. I have learnt that some hospitals use a port instead of an I/V. That isn't normal routine here and not with me. Then the first batch of cytotoxic drugs was introduced. I was advised by a friend who had been through this treatment to suck a sweet. I am glad I listened as I got the most awful metallic taste in my mouth like I had put an old penny or door key in my mouth. Come on, admit it, we have all done it at some time in our lives. The worst was a red-coloured fluid. I don't know if that's the F, the E, or the C. This is nicknamed the red devil. As soon as that went through the I/V, my body went into shock mode. I felt awful and my skin turned a pale grey. It felt like all my peripheral circulation had shut down.

In three hours it was all over, and I was already pee'ing pink.

21

As I am very aware of my body through my endurance sports, I could feel it wasn't right. Possibly some of this was also the side effect of the anti- emetics. I was discharged, and we were collected by my youngest son, Collin.

We went for a walk with the dogs, enjoyed an ice cream and then went back to my son's. Suddenly, a couple of hours later, the sweat began pouring off my head, and I felt really nauseous. It was time to go home. I could deal with any problems better at home. As all my body excretions were now toxic, if I threw up in his home, it would be a real problem. I was feeling yukky, a bit like the first stages of seasickness. Oh yes, me a sailor. Been there, seen it, done that. I have fed the fishes in many seas.

My plan on reaching home was to lay down and relax on the settee. That didn't happen. The curse of Facebook and a very concerned fan club.

I went to bed after taking the dog for a last stroll. I was feeling a bit shivery now, too. I hadn't eaten a proper meal, just some soup, a couple of sandwiches, and ice cream. At 4 a.m. I was awake, burning hot, and very thirsty. I downed a large glass of drink and took another to my bedroom. That was gone by 5 a.m. but sleep came, and I awoke at 8 a.m.

The fact that the next entry in my daybook is a summary of the following seven days speaks volumes.

Lethargy with a capital L. You can liken it to having a

serious hangover. I have had a few of those in the past, too. How much is from the side effects of the anti-emetic and how much is the chemo, I don't know. My notes say the second day was the worst. The list is simple: severe hiccups, constant nausea, acid reflux, and zero appetite. This is where the self-discipline begins to kick in. You feel sick. You don't want to eat or drink. You have to force yourself. The hydration factor is vital. This is where the real battle starts. It's not fighting the cancer but surviving the chemo. Apparently, the oncologists give you not quite enough of the poison to kill you. I'll believe that.

I found strong spicy foods went down okay and didn't threaten to return. Although advised against taking any supplements by the oncology nurse, as my digestive system was still in fair condition, I started each day with a light multivitamin drink. The reason for not taking them being that all bodily systems, including the liver and kidneys, are damaged; therefore, the chance of a vitamin overdose is increased.

On the second and third days, I could not face my usual muesli for breakfast and porridge was definitely a no go. On day five, I felt recovered enough to take a slow stroll into Wommels, a round trip of four kms, to do some shopping.

Being a Tuesday, the fish stall was there and the aroma of frying fish assaulted my nostrils. It smelt good even though I had severe nausea and had to use Primperan, an anti-emetic suppository. There is really nothing like torpedoing yourself first thing in the morning to start your day right!

I bought myself a portion of kibbling which is strips of fish deep fried in batter. I sat down on a bench, ate it, and washed it down with an isotonic energy drink. The latter seemed to help against the nausea. The fish went down exceedingly well and didn't try to swim.

A general picture of how I felt would be about three degrees under par with sudden power outs which indicated horizontal time on the settee. Forget about bed, you won't even make it up the stairs. You just have to rest. Now! You may go to sleep, often not, the power outs lasted anywhere between forty-five minutes to a couple of hours.

By day six, I began to feel reasonable. The low grade constant headache was almost gone, the appetite was still a bit shaky, but the muesli went down and didn't bounce.

I also found out I could sprint again. For several weeks I had been having trouble with kids "knocking dolly out of bed." Yes, I know, I did it too. These kids were pretty rubbish at it but persistent, I'll give them that. It usually started at around 2 p.m. on Friday and went on all through Saturday. It was some older kids, and they were egging on younger kids to do it, too.

The thought of that going on while I was under treatment and not knowing how it was going to affect me, I decided it was time to make an end to it.

As I said, they were persistent so I stood by the door. I saw the hand reaching for the bell through the glass panel and whipped open the door. They ran! Well they had a couple of yards start on me, but I had them both by the scruff of the neck in about thirty yards.

I felt the operation wound during the sprint but bit the bullet. I think that thirteen was a bit old to be playing that silly game.

I frog marched them to their parents so they could explain what they had been doing and for their parents to explain to them that it really was not a good idea at this time.

A week after the first chemo, I was feeling pretty good. My stomach actually said hungry although it was still quite acidy. The plan was to try a run. So in the afternoon, I tried a four x three minutes with two minute pauses. It went okay. I could really feel the wound on the second three- minute run, and my condition seemed to be poor, but a good stretch and some yoga exercises helped. I thought that yoga may have a role to play over the next few months.

Things slowly returned to near normal. My sleep was a bit messed up which wasn't helped by a blackbird stretching his lungs at 5 a.m. each morning.

A Johnny Cash tribute band came to Wommels so I went with Lisa. We both looked mean in our leathers and me with a bandana. I was looking pretty good as yet with no visible signs of what was going on. We had fun, a bit of rocking away on the spot and enjoying a couple of beers. I didn't want to put any more pressure on my liver than it already had to cope with.

Sunday, the 20th, I awoke feeling good. I took Bassie for a stroll and really enjoyed the sun but later in the afternoon, I started feeling a little dizzy which didn't clear up. My mouth is also getting a bit sore, a touch of glossitis, and my appetite remained a bit questionable. There was simply nothing I fancied, but what I ate went down okay. It seemed to be similar to morning sickness on that score, not that I have any personal experience apart from being a dad.

The Monday began as another sunny day. The temptation to go fishing was high, but I was still feeling a little dizzy. My head and beard felt a bit itchy. I rubbed my face and found a mass of my beard attached to my fingers. It was time to get the trimmers out and go extreme. I had been told if you trim your hair short, it helps. So I trimmed my hair and my beard very short.

That evening when I went to bed, I saw that the wound was very inflamed and hot, and I spiked a temp of 38.2. This was probably why I had been feeling dizzy.

Tuesday morning, I was off to my G.P. as instructed by my folders. She suspected an abscess and sent me off to the hospital. They really didn't want to play as I was a chemo patient. I was kept hanging around for several hours until they could get the surgeon out from the operating theatre. She simply wrote me up for antibiotics and told me to make a date with the mammacare nurse on the Thursday.

The antibiotics began to work. It was a cellulitis probably caused by the build-up of lymph in the wound area. It had been drained off a couple of times by the mammacare nurse since the operation but now had been left to try and get it to stabilise.

Now came the reaction that I find really underlines the presence of a Pink Unicorn. I couldn't telephone directly through to the mammacare nurses as I had done before and who, of course, know me. I had to book the appointment through the surgical department receptionist. I made the appointment and the receptionist asked who it was for. I replied me. The telephone line went deathly silent at the hospital end. After about forty-five seconds, the receptionist then confirmed what I had said sounding very flustered indeed. This is the reaction my family and I have become used to.

The Pink Unicorn strikes again.

More Thoughts

During treatment, you tend to muse about things. Cancer means you have to take time out and you have to look after you. Put yourself first. For some, this may be for the first time in their life.

I got to thinking about the amount of time taken from the first discovery in late February. All the hanging about from March 5th until April 11th while it was known that the tumour was malignant, and finally starting chemo on May 9th. That was five weeks to surgery and nine weeks to chemo. You wonder if this time lag will have any effect on the end result. There are also downers that hit you harder than usual. A Facebook friend from the submarine lounge who said she would help me through the treatment when she heard I had been diagnosed with breast cancer, sadly lost the battle herself. She had gone through chemo seven times. She had said no to an eighth treatment.

R.I.P. Sharon. You were a true warrior. At this stage of the game, I had absolutely no idea just how much of a warrior.

Also during this period, you find friends you didn't know you had and other friends run a mile in the opposite direction. It's not their fault. They just can't handle the problem. They want to help you, but they don't know how. The fact is there's nothing much they can really do except stand by helplessly and watch you go through it all. Some husbands have a real problem with this. They have always been there to protect their wife. Suddenly, they can't. They can't fix it. Psychologically, they have failed in their role as a husband and a man.

You also get really hacked off with all the support clichés: "You can fight this," "Get in there and fight," "You are strong," "Have faith!" "Give it to Jesus!" It is all well meant, but while you are still hanging around waiting to start treatment, you can't even begin to fight. Then it just adds to the fear, stress, and frustration. Most of those saying it have no idea what it's about--not even when they have nursed people with terminal cancer as I had done. I certainly had no idea.

When the specialist looks at you wearing that serious face and says, "I am sorry, it's cancer and it's malignant," you crash through into a whole new world.

All your hopes, fears, values, and perspectives get a major reshuffle. The man with the big scythe has just said hello and confronted you with your mortality. Your life will never be the same again. You can never ever go back to how things were.

Even I have my little quirks. I'll talk about Magere Hein as he is called here in The Netherlands or the tall skinny geezer with the big scythe and people losing the fight. There's one word I don't use, that is "death." Call it denial if you like, but it works for me. That is the one rule about this disease and more so the treatment. Whatever gets you through, use it. Many people find religion and pin their faith in their God to get them through. My religious beliefs are mine and don't concern anyone else. I did inform my local Vicar or dominee, as he is called here, as some of the congregation who would see me losing my hair and looking frail and ill might ask him. He put it in the church magazine. Some people prayed for me, others sent me get well cards even though they didn't know me as such. I honestly thank them for this.

A lot of people talk about tunnels and lights at the end. That idea was not right for me. It puts you into a dark place that I find depressing and downright scary. I wasn't in a dark place, I was in a difficult place. Mentally, I used what I know--a long-distance trek through the mountains with a heavy pack on my back. There's a definite destination and a date that you should reach that destination. No one can help you carry that pack. No one can help you walk. They may walk with you and speak words of encouragement to you, but you have to do the walking. The hard days of chemotherapy were climbing steep slopes and fighting strong winds and storms. The good days are walking gently downhill with the sun shining and enjoying the view. I know that if I stop or lay down that heavy pack, I won't get off the mountain.

Sometimes my head was down with the teeth gritted, and I wouldn't talk to anyone, not even go online. I was just concentrating on putting one foot in front of the other. Yes, my head was down, but it wasn't hanging and my eyes were still laughing. Such a challenge I had never known before. I am Jack, and I am a submariner. Magere Hein has got a real fight on.

Round Two

It was now time for the second dose of F.E.C. I got my bloods done and we went up to the ward. Once again, they double-checked when I checked in at reception. It was breast cancer, and I was a man. I had both my daughter and my eldest granddaughter with me this time. That had been my hardest task, having to tell my grandchildren I had cancer. My eldest, Nathalie, is fairly level headed but cloaks her feelings just like her mum and her grandad. My grandson, Melvin, is autistic so it didn't really register in the normal way. My youngest granddaughter, Patricia, just sat there with huge silent tears rolling down her face. That was so heartbreaking. At least I was lucky. I was a grandad that could put his arm around her shoulders and say it would probably be okay. I had a good chance of a cure. Too many grandads are robbed of that, being diagnosed too late. For them, it's just the long goodbye.

The chemo went about the same as the first round. We were given lunch and then walked around the shops a bit before going to Lisa's flat. We also started a new custom and that was to have a Dutch herring after chemo. Again, I was fine up until about 5 p.m. and then the stuff really kicked in, and I started to feel rough. Time to go home to my little dog.

In between on Facebook, I had been invited to join the

breast cancer survivors via an ex-Navy medical branch colleague of mine. A friend of his had read something I had written, and she liked it. It has been extremely useful even though I have been the only man until very recently. The ladies like a "male view" on the subject at times. They also like my "no bull" attitude. It was through them I found malebreastcancer.org, an American site, now the breast cancer coalition. That is both heartbreaking and eye opening to the situation concerning men with breast cancer. The site itself was set up "in memorium" by the children of a man who died from breast cancer. He had been sent home being told there was nothing wrong by various American doctors for eight years. His story is repeated time and time again. If you read the stories, you will cry if you are human, tears of sorrow and tears of anger. A man who died at age forty-two leaving behind a wife and two young children. He, too, had been sent away time and again for eight years before finally a doctor sent him for a mammogram. He had been told repeatedly his discharging nipple was merely a cyst. The same thing also happens in the U.K. and here in the Netherlands. It is vital time wasted and lives needlessly lost. Most of those poor unicorns were fathers and many also grandfathers. Several times I have read "my grandad died of that." Those children were robbed of their grandfathers by an ignorance that is perpetuated by the media.

On the survivors' site, I also learnt that one of the side

effects of chemotherapy was losing your nails. This isn't mentioned in my folders, but too late I had already tapped a finger a bit too hard while messing about and had a "black nail." The advice was to use nail hardener. For me, it didnt work.

Yes, this really is a woman's disease. I was told to use handcrème on my hands, especialy the left, all cuts and scratches to be thoroughly cleaned and covered with a sticking plaster, and to apply lipsyl if my lips began to crack. That, and in general, pampering myself. After losing all my hair, there also came a need for baby powder. Me, a submariner, using foo foo dust? Oh the shame. This disease just isn't right for a man.

The days following the chemo followed the same general format as before except the impact was a bit harder and lasted longer. The energy brownouts were more frequent and lasted longer. My taste had changed from eating crystalised ginger to a complete aversion along with orange juice and oranges. I found "stroop waffles" (a sort of caramel-filled wafer biscuit) helped against the nausea. It was a matter of eat little and often. To try and keep my blood values up, especially iron, I added liver and spinach into my diet at least weekly. As it was natural, if my body couldn't accept it anymore, it would not cause an overdose. I had a hard time convincing my son, Chris. He wanted to help in anyway he could and arrived with a huge pot of super strength multivitamins. He was a little upset when I said I couldn't take them on a daily basis. I am not the expert so if the oncology nurse says no, then it's no, and that was applied to any medicines, even over-the-counter stuff.

By now, I was now 99% hairless with less hair on my body than when I was born. I still had my eyelashes and a wisp of my eyebrows and when half of what was left of my beard fell out, it was time to lose the lot. This time it was day eight before I felt something like normal. A training run was cut down to three x two minutes. The last two minutes were pure purgatory.

Talking of purgatory, there is the chemo smell--the stench emanating from my body. I think the sickly sweet smell of human decomposition sums it up best. It is awful. I expect it comes from all the cells that are dying and breaking down releasing all sorts of toxins.

Chris asked me to come over to his house one day so I walked into Wommels to get the bus. It's only two kms, but the roads were up for repair in Wommels and the usual bus stop was shut. I walked to the next bus stop. Wrong. They had taken Wommels completely out of the route. I walked down to the bypass but found the bypass bus stop was on the other side of Wommels. I had to call Chris to come and get me. I simply couldnt manage the walk back into Wommels. This was hard for Chris to see, let alone me. Not even six kms, and I was dead on my feet. Such things do mess with your mind. The choice is laugh or cry.

Chris was busy repairing my poor motorbike after the crash in February, stripping it down to see what needed replacing and what could be repaired. I was there to help him, but just a few minutes of spanner work, and I would be exhausted and need to rest. Several times he and Chirly had an extra mouth at the dinner table to save me having to cook when I got home. Those little savings of energy are so important especially if you don't have the willpower of an elephant.

Round Three

So just when you are feeling a bit better, it's dose three of the F.E.C. Same routine--go to the hospital, meet my daughter, go to the lab and have my bloods done. These results were sent straight up to the ward as soon as they were ready. Welcomed to the ward, I was shown to my usual room and offered drinks.

And it was I/V time. This time I had to tell them to use a different vein as the last treatment had upset the vein which was still quite sore. They can only use the right arm due to the lymph glands being removed from the left. They musn't even take my blood pressure using the left arm. That really messes them up as most are taught to use the left arm to take the blood pressure.

As usual, we are having fun and generally laughing and messing about as much as anyone can while laid on a bed with a tube hanging out of their arm.

If no one has yet realised, I have a special link with my daughter. This goes back to directly just after her birth. We can read each other. We know when there is something wrong with either of us. It is just a look in the eyes, and we know. "What's up?" "Nothing." "Bull! What's up? Out with it." That goes both ways. It's hard to keep secrets from each other.

After the usual soup and sandwiches around 12:00, it was

time to go. We walked through town as usual, did a little shopping and then went to Lisa's flat, stopping at the fish stall for the herrings. Both my granddaughters love them too. They are supposed to be very healthy. I don't really care. They taste good and go down well. My body seems to want them, and I have learnt to listen to my body. My taste changed once again. I had been drinking a red fruits squash. Now it's a no go. I switched to a tropical mix which went down nicely.

While undergoing chemo, it is vital to drink. Even though I drank quite a bit, it wasn't enough. It made things more difficult as it took longer to flush out the chemo and toxins. This is not just the chemo but the toxins released by the dead cells. Thus, you felt yucky longer. Part of the trouble was that I no longer felt thirsty. I would go for hours before I realised that I hadn't drunk anything. The advice I give to those starting chemo is to spread bottles of water, squash, whatever, all around the house so that seeing one reminds them to drink. It is about this time that I start getting a new side effect. It took almost two weeks to start feeling reasonable after this third and last round of F.E.C. Three of my fingernails are now black from simple knocks.

I did have a day trip out with Lisa and Nathalie. We went to Harlingen and had fun. We came home with a huge bag of ripe mangos. Nathalie had never had fresh mango. Grandad knows how to lead her astray!

In a week, I'll be going for my fourth treatment. This time it's Taxotere. I have been reading some nasty things about this stuff online. The F.E.C. has ten common side effects. Taxotere has double!

July 11th. Taxotere day. After reading the experiences of the ladies on the breast cancer survivors' site, you approach it in a Banzaaii mode. The same kind of feeling as you abseil down a cliff face for the very first time.

The best simile is that the whole cancer thing is a massive roller coaster. Each person's ride is different. The only thing in common is that you step on when you get the first diagnosis. You sit down and hang on for dear life as its clicks up through the waiting period. You have no control. You can't make any plans as you don't know how you are going to be on that day. You can only make an intention. Some people sail through chemo with almost no problems. Others are so ill they even need to be admitted to the hospital. Make any selection of twenty-two side effects at various severities. You can only react to how you are at that moment. Plan for the worst and hope for the best. Live each day as it comes.

For me, that was very true with Taxotere. Bloods done and then up to the ward. They know me and my daughter by now. Made comfortable, the blood results came in and it was all systems go. My Hb, iron, had actually improved a little although by normal standards I had dropped to female values. The white cell count was dropping fast. They had the proverbial glide angle of a brick.

I had made a strict rule that if you had a cough, cold, or whatever, or had been in contact with anyone that was ill, if you care about me, STAY AWAY! A simple cold can put a chemo patient into intensive care or worse.

As it was only one bottle of Taxotere, it was all over and done with quite quickly. I had no immediate reactions to it unlike the red devil. No metallic taste. It is just like the roller coaster; you are left wondering what's coming next. No one can tell you.

Maybe it was the pre-med, Dexamethasone, that kept everything damped down, but I felt okay; a bit of nausea and hiccups but that could also come from the Dexamethasone. Thursday came and went with no problems. Friday came and went, still nothing. Saturday, I was okay at first then started feeling a bit yukky and tired. So I went to bed a bit earlier after taking the dog for his evening stroll.

Oh boy. That night. The pain. I can only imagine it was like an acute attack of rheumatoid arthritis.

Taxotere found every bony injury I had ever had in my life. Every twist, sprain, fracture, or severe bruise. They all hurt. My feet, ankles, and wrists were pure agony. I almost cried with the pain.

I actualy took a painkiller as it was that bad. Oh yes, Taxotere was mean. The symptoms slowly eased off over the next four or five days. Only to be replaced by a sore mouth as it says in the folder. Sore mouth is an understatement! Imagine your mouth is one huge ulcer. Well, that is basicaly what it is. The cell changeover is very fast in the mouth. The replacement cells are killed off so your mouth is simply raw. I really hadn't allowed for this, and it took me two very painful hours to eat a small bowl of muesli.

The next downer was the last hair on my body fell out-- eyelashes and the hair in my nose. My eyes also started streaming with the slightest breeze which meant my nose ran, but without nasal hairs, by the time you realised your nose was running, the drops were already hanging on your lip. This cost me several cups of coffee. My fingertips lost most of their sensitivity. My face and nose felt numb in places, just like I was slightly drunk. I suppose one benefit to ease the pain of my mouth, I got litres ice cream. For a main meal, I had tins of ravioli and soups. I used soft sponges to clean my mouth using alcohol- free mouthwash.

I had both constipation and diarrhoea. This is not good for haemorrhoids. I will not go into literally very gory detail, on top of which my energy levels went through the floor. Total brownout. My breathing became shallow. Just climbing the stairs to my bedroom would leave me breathless.

I went to my son, Chris', home. We were going to work on my bike and his car. The cycle ride into Wommels was tough. The legs just hadn't got it anymore. These are the same legs that did a couple of 200 km cycle tours and legs that ran nine marathons. These are the mental assaults for a man.

While at Chris', I enjoyed a nice salad. I say enjoyed, but the sparkle seemed to have gone from food. I noticed that earlier when Chris and I had a portion of kibling with sauce, it was nice but it seemed flat. About the only good point was that the constant nausea was gone. My fingernails all felt bruised and some were discoloured. I did ask a question online but just got conflicting answers as to how often I should remove and replace the hardner. One person told me their nails were still thin after a year. Yet another trauma in the woman's world.

This was the worst mountain storm so far and there were still two more storms to go.

General Thoughts

It wasn't all bad. Having moved into the little rural village in the summer of 2011, I didn't really know anyone. Many knew me. I was Chris' father, and I was English; so are all of my children, but no one knows it. They moved here when they were young so they learnt the language here and picked up the local accent. They also speak a little of the regional language of Friesian. You can equate that to Cornish.

I had told my next door neighbours of my problem who immediatley offered their help if I needed it. Only once did I need their help, being very independant. I preferred to use my family first, but this time Collin and Chris were away and Lisa doesn't drive. I went to the surgery/pharmacy to get the prescription for my next pre-med only to find the pharmacy was shut. The service had been taken over by a doctor's pharmacy in Wommels. I simply couldn't manage the double journey to drop off the prescription and then return to collect it. I no longer had the strength to walk or cycle eight kms. My neighbour took me in his car. One time a neighbour saw me as I left the supermarket so he took my shopping home for me while I walked home with my dog. There were other little problems to surmount like opening a ring pull can when you have no strength, no feeling in your fingertips, and no finger nails. During the treatments, I also had regular telephone calls from the oncology nurse, visits from the dominee, and my G.P.

My poor G.P. I think she loved to come see me although I confused her, and she wasn't too enthusiastic about my little dog. My positive attitude saw that she always left with a smile on her face. My little dog is everybody's friend and expects a fuss from everyone he sees. From what I have read and learnt over the past months, I realise I am very lucky to have such a G.P. If she hadn't sent me off straight away for a mammogram "just in case," I probably wouldn't be writing this story. I would have been just another "oops, too late" statistic. Another family without a grandad. Another Pink Unicorn lost.

Taxotere 2

Aug 1st. Round five. Again it was the same old routine. I had forgotten to take my Dexamethasone the night before so I took one at 6:30 in the morning as I thought that would be about the level in the blood system. It seemed to work. I met Lisa as usual along with Patricia. It was school holidays. We thought she should see what was going on so such things wouldn't be scary. She was also treated to the soup and sandwiches. Patricia is a wild child. She has A.D.H.D. It all got a bit too exciting for her. The fun got a little extreme. Just because we find the fun in almost everything we can, other people don't; also, others weren't so lucky as me. They were merely fighting for time, not a cure. What we were doing was making what should have been a scary day full of evil portent into a fun day.

Who just lays there and lets someone pump an almost lethal level of poison into your body knowing it will make you sick? That's pretty damn silly for starts.

I have looked at the photos taken on that day and see how bloated I am. Totaly hairless, my skin is sallow and toneless. I haven't really been out in the sun. Even sitting fishing for any length of time is a no go. The skin would be dry and cracked except for the handcrème and simple soap I use. Mind you, I did save money on shampoo and shower gel! That's the secret, looking for the positives. The effects of this were pretty much the same as last time. No side effects showing immediatly after administration, although my appetite was absolute zero that evening.

In the morning I awoke, and my mouth was a bit sore, and the hiccups were back. I did have a little smile. During the night I had been bitten by a mosquito. I looked at the itchy red bite and thought revenge! Strangely, a couple of days later Chris told me about a mosquito that spiraled down and fell dead next to his dinner plate. Twenty-four kms away? Nah, it couldn't be, could it? No matter. You bite me and make me itch, then my blood makes you feel sick. That's pure Karma!

That evening I had a chicken curry as it was still "viable." Again, it tasted flat and that included fresh fruit. I thought the sweet and possibly the sharp taste buds had been knocked out. In the evening, I had a couple of tweaks in my wrists and right ankle. Precursors of things to come? I put an extra folded blanket at the bottom of the bed to keep my feet extra warm. It seemed to help.

August 4th. I am really sad. My taste buds are as good as gone. The sweet/sour being the worst hit. I saw a big, ripe juicy blackberry, popped it into my mouth and nothing, just some tasteless liquid and some pips. A handful of raisins was exactly the same. All I can sense is the texture. Later, I stopped for some chips with mayonnaise at La Bamba's. They serve the best chips for miles around. They may as well have been sawdust in motor oil. Even the glazed carrots I did that evening tasted like nothing.

I had some tinned pineapple. It may as well have been white cabbage as it had a similar texture. If I had been blindfolded, I couldn't have told the difference.

I had pain in my ankles, shins, and wrist. My hands were shaking. The soles of my feet were burning hot. My walking was poor. My legs feel weak. I'm unsteady on my feet and have to take shorter paces. I have neuropathy over much of my body--hands, face, feet, down my arms and thighs.

My next notes are for August 8th and 9th. For the 8th, I simply say "Wow!" Although the breakthrough was gentler because we had tapered off the Dexamethasone, it was still heavy. My mouth wasn't quite as sore. My legs were feeling very weak, my feet felt like I was walking on thick hot sponges. I had pain in the long bones and my ribs, and I had developed a cough. In the afternoon, I was completely wiped out. I was flat for four hours without enough energy even to reach for the camomile tea to ease my mouth. I think a description of flu-like symptoms is the best description followed up with shivering and aching legs. I didn't round the corner until about the 10th of August. I was feeling unbelievably weak. Simply hanging up my washing, a few t-shirts, underwear, and socks, and I was exhausted. My arms were simply dead. After three t-shirts, I was gasping for breath. Seventeen days later, the improvement was still very slow. My legs were still very weak. The cough was more pronounced and also the breathlessness. I did a peak flow which gave me readings of 540, 550, and 550 so no signs of asthma, but when I googled the readings, the results I found said I should be 1.75 meters tall and eighty years old, not 1.83 meters and sixty-four years old. Looks like I will have to dig out the power breathe exerciser and begin daily exercises.

The Last Mountain

August 22nd. I had a review with the mammocare nurses before going for the last dose of chemo. There is a revalidation group at the hospital which they would like me to join. It's to help cancer patients get back to fitness.

After being dragged along by a shitzu and exhausted after a few hundred yards, I think I need it. There is also a psychiatric part attatched to the course. I don't think I really need that as I have no problem with the fact I have cancer. I think after facing Magere Hein with Sue for all those years we were together, he doesn't really worry me. Sue knew she was dying, I knew she was dying, so it was a matter of living while we could. Another factor could be I am still grieving for Sue. Caring for her full-time for those six years and fighting with councils, the benefits offices, and jobcentres, etc. had left me core tired. The constant battles with all the goverment bodies and their bureaucratic hydra to try and get the help we needed did far more damage than the actual physical caring ever did even though I was on my own without any support seven days a week, fifty-two weeks a year and up to twenty hours a day. I was rarely getting three hours' straight sleep at any one time so a small part of me said if it all went pear shaped, I really couldn't give a damn. I could stop fighting, and the pain of her loss would be over. I am glad Sue didn't have to see me go through this. It would have broken her heart.

I had a review in November to remeasure both my arms. They are two cms thicker than the initial measurements. I also had to arrange for the revalidation course. If I could do it, I could probably claim for it the same as taxi transporation from my insurance.

Once on the ward, I got my blood results. Everything had dropped except the thrombocytes. My Hb was 7.2; for a man, that should be about 11. The I/V went okay although it was a bit sore, and we had to reduce the flow. I had remained breathless and coughing. My nose was running like a tap, my skin dry and hands sore. Last dose--what would happen? I just had to suck it and see. It looked like my sleep was going to be hit again.

The oncologist came to see me on the ward. I would only be seeing him for reviews now. Hopefully.

He wanted me to start the Tamoxafin at the same time as the radiotherapy. When we left, Lisa and I stopped for a drink in the hospital restaurant. Strangely, I fancied some orange juice, the first since it all began, and it went down well.

My taste buds were returning at last.

August 25th. My daughter took part in a local road race-- ten km, the same first road race I had run back in 1991. I stood by the finish line waiting for Lisa. Patricia saw the tears rolling down my face and thought I was crying from the emotion of seeing my daughter running. Nah, just the chemo. I was just sad I couldn't do the run with her, but we will run a race together again soon.

The next entry in my daybook is September 6th. The pattern was the same as the previous doses of Taxotere. Everything okay for a couple of days and then all hell broke loose once again. I staggered the Dexamethasone. It made the breakthrough a bit easier. Although the symptoms didn't seem so severe as the fifth treatment, it would have been hard for them to be worse. I felt about one hundred sixty-four, not sixty-four, and that's a sixty-four year old, whom the majority of forty-four year olds would have had trouble keeping up with.

To summarise. I was wheezing like an asthmatic. The slightest exertion had me breathless. A few minutes' work like hanging up some wet t- shirts left me exhausted. My hands were shaking. I kept dropping things as my fingers simply couldn't feel them. Even more fun was attempting to pick them up again. My balance was shot because I couldn't feel my feet properly. I could only walk with a slow shuffling gait, and it was impossible to walk and talk at the same time. Added to which my eyes and nose were streaming like Niagara Falls. To finish off, I was totally hairless and my skin looked awful.

What did I know about chemo when I started? Only that you feel sick and your hair falls out.

I have learnt a whole new respect for all cancer patients everywhere.

With luck, this will be the only time I have to go through this. I can now honestly understand when people say they would rather die than go through it all again.

It's Zapping Time

Radiotherapy: the art of destroying cancer cells with radiation. I suppose in my case, I could look at it as homeopathy, curing like with like.

Knowledge is power. I had no fears about radiation. I knew how I felt after sitting in a reactor compartment half the night with just low-level background radiation. That's why I had been a classified radiation worker. For me, there were no terrors of the unknown.

I did baulk at the idea of starting Tamoxafin and radiotherapy while still recovering from chemo. All attack the immune system, and we were now heading into the cold and flu season. My immune system was already flat. I did raise my doubts online and got all sorts of abuse up to and including being called a quitter.

Sorry, Tamoxafin is an oestrogen suppressant. I am a normal man. I produce very little oestrogen.

To delay it for a week or two while my immune system recovers slightly wasn't quitting. The risk from the action I considered to be minimal. The risk of an infection was greater. That's what I did. I couldn't really find any information about the side effects of Tamoxafin and men. It was mainly confined to the menopausal side effects on women.

I went for an appointment at the Radiological Institute Friesland in Leeuwarden to meet my radio oncologist; another lovely lady doctor. We had a little chat. I told her that I was a former radiation worker and a nurse which made everything so much easier for her.

I was to have thirty-five daily treatments over seven weeks, one week soley on the area of the top or sentinal gland. She warned me that there was a chance the treatment could trigger lymphoedema, a chronic build up of lymph in the affected arm making it swell up like a balloon. Following that, I was marked up ready for treatment. They make skin tattoos on the target area on your back and chest followed by what resembles the runway approach markings in felt-tip pen. The skin tattoos are just small pin points which grow out in a few weeks. The felt tip needed replacing weekly.

I started treatment on September 17th. It was great. My insurance paid for the taxi. Well, I had to pay an initial 92 euros. The idea of the taxi transport is to stop people with a low immune system travelling on public transport. I had no one to drive me. There's no public transport from the village to talk of. Three bell buses in the morning and four in the evening for workers and school kids. Nothing weekends. My motorbike was still in pieces. I couldn't have ridden it anyway in my weakened state. So taxi it was. Most vehicle insurance companies won't cover you anyway while you are undergoing treatment.

The taxi picked me up by my front door thirty minutes before my appointment. I checked in, waited a few minutes before being called in, and removed my top. I assumed the required position, which was a bit difficult as the arm didn't want to go that way. The muscles had tightened and being a man, I don't have that sort of mobilty in my shoulders anyway. For the first few treatments, they covered the area with a wet towel, nicely pre-warmed, to reduce the radiation penetration. They wanted to get the surface cells. Then I went to put my top back on. See you tomorrow. It was all over so quickly, my driver would still be drinking his coffee. Then the thirty-minute journey back home.

I asked my various radiographers if they had ever treated a male breast cancer patient before. None of those I spoke to had. Even the radio oncologist had only seen it once before in her whole career. The staff didn't seem quite as confused by the diagnosis apart from a mild curiosity. I was very impressed with the R.I.F. The place was very busy, yet it was very clean and warm. The staff was friendly, yet professional. Only once there was a delay when Murphy's Law struck; a machine had broken down and there was an emergency patient brought in. That was the only time my driver finished his coffee in peace.

I had several drivers and all sorts of vehicles. One, a young lady, asked me what my treatment was for. There's only one reason you go to the R.I.F., and the taxi company has a contract with the medical insurance company, so I told her. She thought she had misheard me. So I repeated. She was so shocked, we almost ended up in the ditch.

October 20th, eight weeks since I finished chemo. My hair is returning. It's like a fine white peach fluff. All my fingernails are falling off and probably my great toenails. I still have some neuropathy in my fingers and my feet. My walking speed is getting back to normal, and I have tried a couple of gentle runs. I'll only say that they went, but I am an absolute physical wreck. As for my stamina, just fifteen minutes' light work, and I'm exhausted.

The radiotherapy was going okay although I was beginning to burn, and I possibly had lymphoedema. My advice was not to use anything while undergoing radiotherapy so I haven't. No deodorants, no creams, or lotions. They say that radiation therapy makes you tired. I don't know. I felt like I still hadn't recovered from the chemo yet.

My last zap was on October 26th. The taxi firm presented me with a cake. Apparently that's something they do with each "customer." It was touching but what a weird feeling.

The last zap. It was all over. You feel stunned and lost. You have been through all kinds of hell, carved up, poisoned, and zapped with radiation. You have felt like crap for seven months and finally it's over. You can lay down that back pack. Now you can relax and start the recovery. Strangely, you don't feel like partying. Many of my female counterparts tell me they simply burst into tears not knowing why. Some go into a bout of depression. I saw a tick off list for signs and symptoms of P.T.S.D. Most cancer patients could tick off at least four. Yes, cancer is pretty traumatic both physicaly and mentally.

Just before the last treatments at the R.I.F., I had contacted the *Leeuwarder Courant*, a regional newspaper, about my concerns for the situation of men with breast cancer. They were interested and decided to do a story about it. It was during my last week of treatment when they came to see me. We had a chat about it all--the ignorance, the taboo, the shame and embarrasment some men felt, and the complete lack of information. A series of photographs were taken. Fourteen days later the article appeared. It got a middle-page spread of the weekend supplement. Wow! What a photo.

I had just returned home from the R.I.F. when it was taken. It was the last week so the irradiated area was very red, and I had been freshly marked up with felt tip. I don't know how the photographer did it, but he captured something very special with his camera, something spiritual. Many people found the photo very confrontational. My daughter simply looked at it and burst into tears. Facebook banned it!

I became a celebrity in my village and far beyond. Ladies

who also had the disease stopped to talk to me in the street. They treated me like one of the girls. They felt they could talk freely with me; a man that could actually understand what they had gone through. Many applauded my courage to be open about it. Personally, I find nothing courageous about it.

The word needs to be put out there to stop men from dying needlessly, to make people realise breast cancer isn't just a woman's disease, and to make some doctors think again. A top specialist at a medical conference actualy stated that men could not get breast cancer. This year there will be 500 American, 100 British, 25 Dutch, and 10 Swedish gravestones that all say he is wrong. If my standing up and baring myself, in all senses of the word for all to see, can save just one life, I will have achieved my goal. Strangely enough, at about the same time I did my story, another Dutchman living in the south did his story in the *Algemeen Dagblad*. In England, three men did their stories in the *Daily Mirror*. So five of us in total. Two had initially been told by their doctors there was nothing wrong. The lump was nothing to worry about. That is a 40% error. That is not acceptble.

December 14th. My fingernails are a mess. I have lost seven of the ten. I still have neuropathy in my fingers and my feet. My energy is returning slowly. I don't need to lay down so often in the afternoon or evening. If I try to do any work with some tempo, it doesn't last very long. Simply sweeping up some fallen leaves in the yard was a killer, but at least I could hang up the wash without having to take a pause. Alas, my suspicions during week four of radiotherapy were right. I have developed lymphoedema, and I let it get quite bad. Not realising the importance of the condition, I resembled a left-handed Popeye. I needed a lymphoedema specialist. She was not happy with me. I ended up in a pressure bandage from shoulder to fingers and massages twice weekly for several weeks. This eventually reduced to weekly, and then I swapped to an elastic sleeve and glove. It was going to be a long job to get it stable. Simply, I had left it too long before getting treatment. The lymphoedema will be a permanent factor in my life. No needles and no blood pressure to be taken from that arm. Long flights can be a problem for which I must definitely wear my sleeve and glove. Long repetitive arm movements are over so I can forget kayaking or rowing.

Like many women do, I piled on weight. Somewhere around seven kilos. That seems to be the average. The main thing is that I am alive, and it looks like I will remain that way for a while yet. I did try some running which I stopped again. My first two minutes' attempt was 1.5 minutes with me hanging on the school fence. At a much lower tempo, I could just manage three x two minutes. A later attempt gave me a slightly higher tempo and more distance covered. My condition was terrible. Whatever, we will see. I could now cycle to Wommels and back without dying and even walk it at a fair tempo carrying shopping on the return. Mind you, I did have a cup of coffee in the supermarket before the return journey.

I was getting there--onward and upward. I am going to do the Herstel and Balans course for revalidation. This course is run by the Antonius Hospital for cancer patients. I need proper guidance to get fit again.

Herstel and Balans
Or in English, Revalidation

January 2013. I have signed up to do the Herstel and Balans course run by the Antonius Hospital. It seems to be a wise move. It is run by physiotherapists who make an individual plan for each person. The course also contains ergonometry and psychiatry. I know the risks of trying to do too much too soon. Much of the cost of the course would be covered by my insurance. I had followed the advice of my mammacare and oncology nurses. Curiously enough, all the group are post breast cancer. My son, Collin, let me borrow his Honda 400 motorcycle. It was winter, and he wouldn't be riding. He still had to get his motorcycle license anyway.

My wicked sense of humour was doing gymnastics as I walked into the room wearing my leather jacket--seven ladies and me, a man. A biker and a foreigner. Now how scary is that!! Pity, I was the last to arrive and the oncology nurse had already warned them about me, but there was still some apprehension among the ladies. The course comprised of two hours in the gymnasium twice a week and an hour of either psychiatry or ergonometry.

It was on the course we learnt about chemo brain. I had read about it. The first trick was to learn and remember each others' name. Seven names that sounds easy. It isn't, not with chemo brain. It is a real phenomenom, something to do with concentration. They don't know the exact cause, but it may be through the chronic exhaustion. Things just don't get processed by the brain properly and get "lost," so we were stood in a circle and had to call a name and throw a ball to that person. Great, there you are struggling to get the names right, and then you learnt just how messed up your hand/eye coordination was. That was followed by the condition tests. Those started with walking up and down the gym at increasing tempos. First, very slow building up to a jog trot. Only two of us made it to the jog trot. The others dropped out at various stages. Then, it was on the exercise bikes with slowly increasing resistance. I was the strongest on most of the machines although a couple I could not do because of the lymphoedema. I did try the rowing machine but inside five minutes, it was already wrong! It felt like someone had filled my arm with liquid concrete.

I was the second oldest on the course. One of the ladies was a couple of months older. The first day it was all very quiet and still very much, shall we say, inhibited. Three of the ladies wore wigs. I wore a bandana being a biker, but mainly because it was cold without my thatch and not out of the embarrassment of being bald.

The next lesson in the gym was a different story. Seven

ladies all chattering away. The funniest part was when we all stood in a group in the gym ignoring the physio and comparing our fingernails. Each thought they were the only ones to lose their nails. It was the first real chance to get together and compare notes. I became accepted as one of the girls. Nothing was taboo. Nothing was left unsaid because I was a man.

More than once I came close to blushing.

From that day, the group became known as the hen house (kippenhok), and I was the cockerel (De Haan).

The ergonometry was interesting. It showed just how much energy we waste each day, energy that we cancer patients simply don't have anymore. The lessons once again were aimed at the woman's world-- washing, cooking, cleaning, vacuuming, and making beds. The psychiatry was a different matter.

It was a form of group therapy. We talked. I thought I was pretty okay about having cancer. I accepted it as a fact of life. Even I found I had a couple of minor hang-ups. A couple of the ladies had some real problems. One started crying and soon there were three all in tears. Each found the pain and fear they had pushed away and not dealt with. It was difficult seeing all the pain and fear coming loose, but we all managed to put the problems into the right boxes in the end. With that came a growing confidence among the ladies. Halfway through the course, the wigs were gone.

During this time, I had a little scare. My right nipple became sore and remained so, just to pressure. I wasn't sure if I could feel anything or not. I still had neuropathy in my fingertips. Was I feeling a small lump or was it just the numbness in my fingertip I was feeling? My review was brought forward, and I was sent for a mammogram. It came back clear--nothing seen.

I had been talking to an Indian doctor who had two male patients and both had bilateral breast cancer. This is a little cloud that each breast cancer patient, in fact, all cancer patients, live with. The weight you are losing. Is it your diet working or something more sinister? That niggling pain which won't go? There is always that little dark cloud on the horizon.

The gym work we split into two groups with one group going onto the fitness machines. First twenty-two minutes on the bikes, each working to their programme, and the programme being altered as each progressed. Then it was working on our back and stomach muscles, our leg muscles, arms, and shoulders. I had to be careful on the arms. The other group did games. So much was on regaining our coordination. Running around pylons with a table tennis ball balanced on a table tennis bat. Playing badminton, Jeu de boel, basketball and volleyball using balloons, and badminton using balloons. There was also circuit training combining several of these exercises. Later on in the course as our condition improved, we went out and did Nordic walking. For me, they had a little difficulty judging my fitness level as I was on a beta blocker so my heart rate was suppressed.

Personally, I am glad I did the course. It got my fitness going in the right direction and learnt where I had problems to work on sorting issues I didn't even know I had. Most of all, we became a team supporting each other. Three of us have lymphoedema and are seeing the same specialist. Several times one of us would be waiting for treatment as another finished treatment. It was a great group of brave ladies, and we have remained in contact with each other giving each other support when it's needed.

The course was quite tough, but it was fun. We made it fun. I like to think I was a bit instrumental in that. The physios said that we were one of the best groups they had to date. One instance was in the gym. We had to do silly walks; not quite Monty Python but close. All was going fine until it was, "Walk like a model on a cat walk." Well that was fine for the ladies. There is no one that can do camp like "Jack," I made Dennis Norden look macho! One of the physios simply lost it with a beetroot face and others were laughing so hard they almost had a little accident! I had a chuckle too.

Laughter is the best medicine ever. If you look back to the previous October when my shitzu, Bassie, was dragging me, a six-foot tall marathon runner, around the village. I had a choice to laugh at the irony or cry; I laughed. Here I was, five months later on the road to recovery getting fit again and understanding some of the restrictions of my new life, including chemo brain. I will lose a word. Being bilingual, often I can find the word in one language but not in the other. One of the ladies was talking about her husband who is diabetic. He had lost his foot. She was talking about the awful smell of the infection. I knew what it was in Dutch: witvuur. It took me thirty-two hours to find the word "gangrene" in English. Names, I am terrible with. If I put something down without concentrating, it will take ages to find it again. I really could forget my head if it wasn't screwed on. Some cancer patients have a problem with this for a year or two, but for others, it seems to be more permanent. Seven or eight years on, and they still have a problem. Well, yes, chemotherapy must also attack the neural pathways otherwise there would be no neuropathy to the hands and feet.

The course has been a great help to us all in dealing with the physical and psychological effects of cancer. I think that all hospitals should run such a course. Sadly, they don't and so often I read of cancer patients who are virtually dropped after the end of their treatment's last dose. Bye, and see you for a review in six months. There they stand, total wrecks both physcially and emotionally. Who is there to help them? Sorry, but if you haven't walked the walk, you cannot understand. It doesn't matter who or what your relationship may be. In fact, partners were invited to some of the Herstel and Balans sessions so the partners could understand some of what was being done.

The After Life

Things were going quite well, very slowly improving. My runs were slowly improving, but my reserve energy was missing. If I pushed things, then I could easily wipe myself out for two days. An hour's physical work was about the maximum.

In late March 2013, I got a letter from the jobcentre stating that as I hadn't signed on as looking for work, they had a meeting. Next month, April, they were going to reduce my benefits. I am still registered sick, and it's two weeks to my 65th birthday. This was my last run-in with the bureaucratic hydra. I phoned the gentleman whose name was signed on the letter. With great difficulty, I was polite and told him I had received the letter and was rather upset by it. I asked for an appointment with him to discuss it. Apparently, because I had phoned him, I could forget about the threat. He refused point blank to make an appointment to discuss it. I asked him if he had read my file. He waffled. I told him to read my file and then to call me back. He stated, in a very high-handed bureaucratic way, that he didn't think he would be able to call me back that day but would see. Two hours later my phone rang. Never before have I heard such a stream of apologies. Blah, blah, this letter should never have been sent, etc. Terribly sorry, blah. I told him it was a bit stupid sending such a thing as I would be retiring in just two weeks' time. I also suggested he read people's files before sending out such letters in the future. Do you really think "they" had a meeting about me? I hope he learnt from it and realises how lucky he was he hadn't had a face-to-face meeting.

I am now happily retired. Just removing that sort of aggro rubbish from my life is fantastic. The amount of aggro cancer patients have to deal with from both employers and work agencies, i.e., jobcentre, is unbelievable.

You need to go through the chemotherapy and radiation to really understand the complete lack of energy we are faced with. It is not like a broken leg--six weeks all better. Talking to other breast cancer patients, I have learnt it can take years before they feel "right" again. It isn't being lazy. Six months after treatment, and I couldn't manage a ten km run; that used to be a warm-up trot. So much for my dream of the Terschelling marathon. It will happen, but it's going to take a long time. In the meantime, I am taking my pills and going to my reviews and getting my mammograms. So far all is going well. My joints tend to hurt a bit which is a common side effect from the Tamoxafin. I still have slight neuropthy in my fingertips and both my feet which messes up my balance.

My hike through the Scottish mountains, the West Highland Way, was successful but raised the question of lung damage from the radiation. This was confirmed by the radiologist/oncologist. Apparently, the top of the frontal lobe and part of the middle lobe have been fried. If I understand correctly, it is the pleura which acts like shrink plastic so those parts of my lung cannot function properly. It was weird trying to push myself up those mountains. My heartrate was okay and would recover quickly, but I just couldn't power up those hills. My lungs wouldn't provide the required oxygen.

At the end of the walk, I did have a scare. Me and my boys camped wild and had a campfire. Getting wood for the fire, I managed to get a foul rotten wood splinter in my left hand. Normally, no problem. I found it in the daylight the next morning, but already there was massive infection around it. Yes, problem. I have no lymph glands in my left arm to fight infection. I had to get that splinter out and get rid of that infection even if it meant going to the local hospital. A filthy splinter was, in fact, a serious problem. Luckily, I had a sharp safety pin in my small first-aid kit and some disinfectant with which I managed to dig the splinter out and clean the whole thing up. Next time, I will wear a leather glove when collecting wood! Cancer is a major learning curve. It is a gift that keeps on giving.

The Birth of a Pink Unicorn

It happens when a man hears those words, "It's breast cancer, and it's malignant." For me it was 5th March 2012. That's when the old me vanished, and the new me came into being. There is no going back, only forward. It's a learning curve. I was one of the chosen few.

You learn just how strong you really are. You learn who your real friends are. You learn about your family relationships. You learn about the world around you, your workmates, your bosses. You get a whole new appreciation for life. You get a whole new set of perspectives. You have to learn to carry on with restrictions such as lymphoedema, neuropathy, and chemo brain; for the ladies, a chemically-induced menopause. You learn to live with our little paranoia; that little dark cloud that hangs on our horizon, the cloud called cancer, and the constant fear that it may return. A persistant cough, a niggling pain that won't go. Losing weight…is it? We have looked into the gaze of Magere Hein. We know we are mortal. Each time we read of someone losing the fight, we hurt a bit more as we know what that fight is like. Cancer respects no one--young or old, rich or poor, man or woman, black or white, God fearing or Athiest--no one is immune. There are many causes of cancer, some real, some mythical, genetic, or hormonal environmental. It needs something to irrritate the cell in such a way it divides the nucleas as well. Radiation will do it, some chemicals will, even exhaust fumes. Apparently, drinking out of plastic bottles where a certain chemical has leached from the plastic in the same way that lead poisoning became endemic. My generaration of London school kids all had mild lead poisoning.

There is no right or wrong way to fight cancer, just your way. Whatever gets you through is good. Some people will get religion and find support there. Some see it as a trial. Some see it as a punishment. It doesn't matter. Only surviving matters. If you are fit and have a whacky sense of humour, it seems to help.

Some friends will support you, others will run away unable to face the truth of your mortality. It's too scary. Marriages will get stronger or fall apart. It is a cruel disease which affects all touched by it permanently. No one is left unchanged.

I ask the question. What have Dusty Springfield, Olivia Newton John, Kylie Monogue, Peter Criss (rock drummer), Robert Roundtree (actor), Montel Williams (TV presentor), and I have in common? The answer? We all had breast cancer. Some people will then look and find four singers and decide singing causes breast cancer or maybe the celebrity bit could be a cause, but then I am neither a singer nor a celebrity even if I have had my fifteen minutes of fame. Statistics can prove or disprove many things. Some people panic as a percentage of their type of cancer relapses and recurs. My answer is my chance was 1 in 100,000 of getting breast cancer. Try not to worry about the numbers as you can't do anything unless it does relapse and if it doesn't relapse, then what? None of us are ever the same. We all changed. Our perspectives are different.

I like the new me. It takes a little getting used to. It can be fun being a Pink Unicorn watching people trying to comprehend a man with breast cancer and seeing their world collapse around them. To see them wondering how a man gets a woman's disease. People ask me if I am cured. I dont know. I tell them to ask again in five years after diagnosis. I hope to be here to answer, but there are no guarantees. I ride my motorcycle, I am back running and trying to get fit, trying to lose the weight I put on. I try and see my friends and family both in The Netherlands and the U.K. I make each day count.

So live, laugh, and love. No one is promised tomorrow. Not even Pink Unicorns.

Review

Four years ago today, I went under the knife removing the tumour in my left nipple and my axilliary lymphatic glands.

The situation concerning acknowledgement of male breast cancer remains. The attitude of breast cancer, now formerly breakthrough cancer, remains the same. The latest campaign is to stop women dying from breast cancer now! And men then? Their answer is we are doing research, but how much research will tell men they need to check their pects just like their wives do?

Last year I climbed Ben Nevis on my 67th birthday, and then we walked the great glen from Fort William to Inverness. In September, I took part in the Viking Colour run in Arnhem, a seven km mud run with twenty-four obstacles. I finished and was even helping competitors half my age with the obstacles. Although, I did get a little bit of a cold afterwards.

After that, my lungs seemed to go down hill, my cough ever present since chemo, got worse, as I would become breathless doing a short walk. I didn't feel ill, just not right. I was running but it wouldn't go well. That's when that little black cloud grows. Add to that, sadly one of my chickens from Herstel and Balans lost the battle.

I came up for review by the oncologist and told him of the

problem. He took it seriously and referred me for a chest x-ray and lung MRI. The latter, on the chance I had an embolism, another risk from the Tamoxafin.

So sitting waiting outside the lung specialist with my daughter, out comes the specialist, "Mrs. Herbert." I said, "Try Mr., but you were close. Confusion." "But I read breast cancer!" That's one battle that is far from over. I politely educated the specialist about the situation concerning male breast cancer. Nothing was found in the MRI. They did a histamine test—nothing, no reaction. But in between, I had caught another cold and hit it with everything including the immune boosters. Wow, finally the thick wallpaper paste I had been coughing up for months turned colour. Pretty shade of green. My breathing started to improve. I felt better. My thoughts are that I had a mild chest infection from the Viking run which, while not kicking in, combined with the damaged lung, dragged me down. Another scare gone.

I am training for a marathon in June. I don't expect a record, just hope to finish. I have also been asked to join in a twenty-four-hour relay walk for a Dutch cancer organisation.

The lymphoedema continues in my left arm and where they "burnt" my vein with the second dose of F.E.C. red devil, I now have adhesions and that vein is no longer viable. Both problems are being treated by my lymphoedema specialist. Initially, I went to a local physiotherapist to get the right arm treated. I told her that I thought the cause was through chemo, and she asked what cancer. It was the usual routine with the physio looking at me doubtfully and saying, "Breast cancer? Well, I suppose it's possible." This was a fully trained and experienced physio. Both the arm conditions are permanent as is the remaining neuropathy in my feet and fingertips and the diminished balance. My joints still creak from the Tamoxafin, and my eyes still stream in a light breeze. I still run out of energy, but I am still here living each day, valuing each day running, motorcycling, sailing, and demanding much from my body, but the biggest fight is fighting to get us Pink Unicorns recognised.

While selecting a cancer charity to donate to for the marathon, I checked out the list on BT/My Donate. Two-thirds of the breast cancer charities specify women. While searching for a sponsor for this book, I only got a reply to my emails from one cancer organisation, Pink Ribbon N.L., who is unable to sponsor, but will promote the book. To those organisations and charities that ignore us Pink Unicorns, I have only this to say:

Breast cancer is not a "woman's" disease. It kills men too.

Alan Herbert. E.N./R.G.N rtd

"You Are in the Lead Foundation."

Initiative for starting the Foundation, 'Jij Speelt de Hoofdrol' ('You Are in the Lead'), was taken by two sisters, Sabine Wernars (ex-breast cancer patient) and Saskia Koopmans (her sister), during Spring 2015. Because all public manifestations, workshops, summits, and publications concerning breast cancer are easily described as top-down information stream(s) dominated by medical specialists, hospitals, family doctors, and nurses from both hospitals as well as medical aid at home, the Foundation wanted the breast cancer symposium to be organized from patients for patients.

Medical information does not cover nor support the whole picture. Patients and ex-patients of breast cancer, male and female, expire and/or suffer a far greater spectrum of non-medical issues like social events, living circumstances, capabilities in living a normal life and within that life recapturing and/or continuing a (normal) professional life, executing their profession, and so on, as compared with 'only' medical aspects of the disease patients have to cope with.

Enlightening a few of them, i.e., late consequences of (chemo)therapy, brain functions becoming unpredictable, and therefore unexpectedly behaving not as they used to do, uncertainty of life, physical and mental conditions causing unusual and unexpected fatigue, not to be taken serious any longer in normal social functioning in private, at work, and in a variety of social circumstances and/or happenings.

The two sisters decided to publically organize events, actions, and publishing information to create respectable awareness concerning such non-medical needs of (ex)-breast cancer patients, male and female. In order to do so, Saskia and Sabine created the non-profit Foundation, 'You Are in the Lead' ('Jij Speelt de Hoofdrol').

18395253R00050

Printed in Great Britain
by Amazon